It is the previous song. I am not forgetting it.

mpT
MODERN POETRY IN TRANSLATION

The best of world poetry

No. 2 2022
© *Modern Poetry in Translation* 2022 and contributors

ISSN (print) 0969-3572
ISSN (online) 2052-3017
ISBN (print) 978-1-910485-33-0

Editor: Clare Pollard
Managing Editor: Sarah Hesketh
Digital Content Editor: Ed Cottrell
Finance Manager: Deborah De Kock
Creative Apprentice: Dom Green
Design by Brett Evans Biedscheid
Cover art by Amani M
Typesetting by Libanus Press

Printed and bound in Great Britain by Charlesworth Press, Wakefield
For submissions and subscriptions please visit www.modernpoetryintranslation.com

Modern Poetry in Translation Limited. A Company Limited by Guarantee Registered
in England and Wales, Number 5881603 UK Registered Charity Number 1118223

Modern Poetry in Translation is grateful to those who have supported the
Focus on Somali Poetry, particularly Kayd Somali Arts & Culture, and the
Let's Create Jubilee Fund.

Supported using public funding by
LOTTERY FUNDED | ARTS COUNCIL ENGLAND

MODERN POETRY IN TRANSLATION

The Previous Song:
Focus on Somali Poetry

CONTENTS

Focus

Reviews

EDITORIAL

This editorial is my last. It's five years since I got this dream job, editing one of the best poetry magazines in the world, but now feels like the right time to hand it over to someone else – especially when that person is Khairani Barokka, a truly brilliant poet, translator and activist who has taught me so much. It has been a wonderful, chaotic, terrifying, beautiful, intense five years, and much of it already seems like a dream – from a thrilling trip to Latvia in my first month on the job, through the panicky blur of the early days of the pandemic.

Having a different focus each issue means I've always had so much to learn, which has been both nerve-wracking and an honour. From interrogating our environmental impact for I *Have not Known a Grief Like This: Focus on Extinction*, to discovering the huge diversity of poetries in Britain for *Our Small Universe: Focus on the Languages of the United Kingdom*, each issue has been an education. I want to thank everyone who has helped me, including the board and team at MPT – especially Sarah, Ed and Debbie; our current chair Andrew (who took over from the much-missed Chris Meade); our wonderful typesetter Susan at Libanus Press, our proofreader Katy, and cover-designers Jenny and Brett. Thanks, too, to our friends at The Queens College, previous editors David, Helen and Sasha, and all the hundreds of other poets, translators and reviewers who have shared their expertise so generously.

With each issue, I've discovered writers I will continue to read and cherish – the LGBTQ+ Focus, *The House of Thirst*, stands out for introducing me to Norman Erikson Pasaribu, Marieke Rijneveld and our future translator-in-residence Soje amongst others. There have been language firsts for MPT – Torwali, Zoque, Yap, Belau, Mè'phàà, Sumerian, Maori, BSL – and new forms to discover, such as the Zo, the Duet, the Licko, the Englyn. I've loved working with guest-editors, and *Origins of the Fire Emoji: Focus on Dead [Women]*

Poets stands out as another highlight. Contributing towards a feminised canon has in many ways been a theme of my editorship, and it has given me deep pleasure to publish previously under-translated female poets such as Enheduanna, Gwerful Mechain, Else Lasker-Schüler, Marie Under, Simone Weil, Nahui Olin, Gisèle Prassinos, Pita Amor, Noriko Ibaragi and, in this issue, Tove Ditlevsen and artist Meret Oppenheim. (You may have noticed all the cover artists I have commissioned have been women too!)

Magazines allow you to react quickly to news. To say 'yes' when people come to you with urgent work. We have been able to give space to Dalit, Uyghur and Rohingya poetry, and, in this issue's pages, *MPT* has brought together voices from the region all writing in response to the invasion of Ukraine. It has been a privilege to share this platform with such brave writers. And what other publication would have a roll-call that includes (forgive the name-dropping) such international talents as Simone Atangana Bekono, Legna Rodríguez Iglesias, Joy Harjo, Polina Barskova, Toon Tellegen, Maria Stepanova, Jan Wagner, Hubert Matiúwàa, Carolyn Forché, Ribka Sibhatu, Marilyn Hacker, Natalia Toledo, Valzhyna Mort, Sawako Nakayasu, Doireann Ní Ghríofa, Shivanee Ramlochan, Stephanie Burt and Azita Ghahreman (not to mention Brecht, Lorca and Sappho)?

I fell in love with Somali poetry many years ago, whilst co-translating Asha Lul Mohamud Yusuf with Maxamed Xasan 'Alto' and Said Jama Hussein, so I'm very glad that my last issue has a Somali focus. Thanks to Ibrahim Hirsi, Martin Orwin, W.N. Herbert, the Poetry Translation Centre, and Hanna and Ayan at Kayd for their help. And a special thanks to Said Jama Hussein, whose knowledge and passion are an inspiration to so many involved in this focus, and to whom it is dedicated.

I will miss editing *MPT*, of course, but am excited to read future issues, and know I will continue to learn from them under Khairani Barokka's care – to be astonished, moved, thrilled and challenged by what poetry in translation can be.

Clare Pollard

MONA KAREEM

Translated by Sara Elkamel

Running through Mona Kareem's three Arabic collections of poetry is an undeniable solitude, captured in portrait after portrait of the poet herself, of nameless cities, and of women protagonists who seem to have been forsaken by the world. Presented in a remarkably lyric voice, Kareem's work holds up mirrors – of varying degrees of lucidity – to the many selves, as well as the bodies, of her subjects. The images that we see reflected strike a memorable balance between the visible and the conceptual, the tangible and the surreal.

The poems I have translated from *What I Sleep For Today* (Nova Plus Publishing and Distribution, 2016), namely 'Souvenirs' and 'Perdition', illustrate the poet's intentional conflation of the body and the world around it – both material and immaterial. Everything becomes a body – has a body – in her poems, even the poem itself. The ocean has an asphyxiating larynx, the speaker's eye is an abyss, and 'the poem lays crucified | over the notepad's knees'.

Written more than a decade earlier, while Kareem was still a teen, the poem 'Cities Dying Every Day', from the collection *Absence with Amputated Fingers* (Dar Sharqiyat, 2004), is a kind of elegy for cities. Like many of her poems, this one presents us with an individual experience in an indifferent, or perhaps even an unkind, city – one that wishes to excavate even our lungs. The speaker here, and recurrently across her oeuvre, seems to be in a state, at once, of terror, and of extreme loneliness; she is abandoned even by autumn.

Cities Dying Every Day

The roads are cavernous,
ravaged by night
and the drunkards...

I will not fold these maps;
it might dent my country's nose,
prompting a plundering of popular pockets
for emergency plastic surgery.

Another blood cell treads
along my artery's narrow bridge –
will the Disease Police intercept it?

Spring lies in my left brain,
but what of autumn?
It is possible it has divorced me,
after inhabiting my entire life?

Inside every tent
is a child who emerges
out of its mother's desert and into another desert
and then another...

Breathe,
leave the task of lung excavation to us.
Breathe,
let Narcissus depart your soul.

Tons of dust
shroud our veins,
but it is incomparable to the dust
that shrouds our smiles.

Many cities die every day;
I myself have died when Sumer decided
to surrender its throne.

Asia
for the millionth time, dons a coat
of wars –
as our lives transform
into aging droplets.

Perdition

Roses take their own life
above the rim of my bed
as my mother
tries to tuck me into the desert of life

◆

In the courtyard of my soul
is a small devil;
a newborn

◆

Another ship
asphyxiates
the ocean's larynx

◆

The moon spills a cloud
into the sky's breast

◆

Ideas drown in a spasm
and the poem lays crucified
over the notepad's knees

◆

The night is strangled
by a choker of stars

◆

A tear
attempts martyrdom
out of my eye's abyss

Souvenirs

It has been a long time since I cut my hair.
A year, precisely.
Now, my memory swells;
its heft fatigues my head.

MERET OPPENHEIM

Translated by Pamela Robertson-Pearce

The Swiss artist Meret Oppenheim was born in 1913 in Berlin. Moving to Paris as a young woman in the early 1930s was pivotal to her artistic development. It was also in Paris that she started writing poetry, mainly in German but also in French. Her first poem, 'For you, against you', was written in the Café du Dôme, where she met her friends Max Ernst, Marcel Duchamp, Alberto Giacometti, Jean Arp and André Breton. 'The dew on the rose' may relate to Man Ray's photographs of her, which she viewed as a collaborative work ('She kept her pale flesh | Her wax | Black and white').

She was first known as a Surrealist, most famously for her objet d'art, the fur-lined teacup titled 'Le Déjeuner en fourrure' (1936), becoming a role model for women artists. Her close lifelong friends included Leonora Carrington and Leonor Fini. The themes and events explored in her wide-ranging art also figure in her playful poetry: her creative crisis and transformation, Paris of the Surrealists, Jungian psychology, Nature, feminism and androgyny.

I first saw Meret Oppenheim's work as a young child at her retrospective at Moderna Museet in Stockholm. Later, when I was an art student at St Martin's in London, I met her in person. We became friends and discussed making a biopic on her life and work. My film, *IMAGO: Meret Oppenheim* (1988), tells her story entirely in her own words, drawn from her letters, diaries, poems and other writings which I translated from the German and French. I think her work is timeless and important not only for its Surrealist connection but particularly for its own landscape and mythology.

Four Poems

I feel how my eye turns towards the forests and the moon.
I feel my compass pointing towards the nourishing proverbs.
But my beautiful crocodile.
My crocodile out of heart,
Where does your pride go?

For you, against you
Throw all the stones behind you
And let the walls loose.
To you, on you
For one hundred singers above you
the hoofs run loose.
I delight in my mushrooms
I am the first guest in the house
And let the walls loose.

The dew on the rose
Who touched it before
Before the night?
She kept her pale flesh
Her wax
Black and white
One sees her again in the clouds
Eating marzipan.

Finally!
Freedom!
The harpoons fly.
The rainbow is floating in the streets,
Only overshadowed by the distant humming of the giant-bees
Everyone loses everything, which they, oh so often,
have overflown in vain.
But: Genevieve:
Stiff
Standing on her head
Two meters above the ground
Without arms.
Her son Realm of Pain:
Wrapped into her hair.
Small fountain.
I repeat: small fountain.
Wind and cries in the distance.

TWO CI

Translated by Helen Bowell and Amanda Wong

Li Yu (937–978) was the ineffective King of the Southern Tang Dynasty and an early ci master. When his country fell to the invading Song Dynasty, Li and his family were captured and lived under their new rulers' surveillance. This poem deals with that imprisonment and longing for home in a past, happier time. It is also said that this poem cost Li his life: the Emperor felt it suggested Li was not a loyal subject and Li was poisoned to death soon after.

Li Qingzhao (1084–1155) is often cited as China's 'greatest' female poet. She was born into a family of scholar-officials during the Song Dynasty, when women would reportedly burn their poetry rather than have people know they were writing – so Li's success was (and has been for centuries) an anomaly. She had a happy marriage for many years, which tragically ended when her husband died during another war between the Jin and Song Dynasties. Her writing, including this ci, then took a sadder turn, focusing on heartbreak and loneliness. Li's poem is famous for its repetition, which we've tried to reflect as naturally as possible in the English (for instance, it begins: 寻寻觅觅，冷冷清清，凄凄惨惨戚戚).

Both poems are well-known ci, a kind of poetry which reached its zenith during the Song Dynasty. All ci are written to fit existing tunes and tonal patterns, and ci titles reference the music rather than the contents of the poems (such as 'Ci to the tune of Slow Sounds'). Though ci were originally sung at bars and parties, they are now very much part of the Chinese literary canon.

LI YU

Ci to the Tune of Yu the Beauty / Concubine Yu

How much more of this spring blossom, this autumn moon?

How many times like this have I seen?

The east wind blew into my room again last night.

I start thinking of home's bright moon and can't bear it:

all the balustrades and jade steps the same,

only the rosy faces yellowed with age.

Ask a gentleman how many times his heart can break.

Count the drops in the river, rushing east in the Spring.

LI QINGZHAO

Ci to the Tune of Slow Sounds

I'm looking, looking out. It's cold and clear and I'm alone.
When the weather changes like this, it's hard to keep well.
How could this bland wine jacket me from the cold, the night, the wind?
It's clear and cold. Wild geese fly past. We used to be friends.

Who would pick these old gold chrysanthemums now?
I'm looking, looking out. When will night come?
The sky mists the phoenix tree. By evening, it'll drip and drip and drip.
It's clear and cold. Standing here, *sorrow* isn't enough.

LOUKY BERSIANIK

Translated by Olivia McCannon

The Québécoise poet Louky Bersianik wrote *Kerameikos* (1987) at the height of Cold War tensions. Her work anticipates 'Anthropocene' concerns, attending to what connects social and ecological justice, patriarchy and kleptocracy, technosphere and biosphere. Kerameikos is a Bronze Age Athenian necropolis. Bersianik's starting point was the Attic tomb of Hegeso, a marble stele showing two women looking together at an unidentifiable object: 'a secret offering kept safe for future generations'.

The poems of the sequence translated here, 'Ruins of the Future', speak to today with their resistance to necropolitical power structures and ideologies that enshrine destruction and finitude. Here and elsewhere in her writing, Bersianik writes back from a future shaped by the flourishing of alternatively civilising, feminist ways of being.

Such a structural opposition, between a patriarchal status quo and a disruptive presence in the feminine, presents in the French as the interplay between the masculine and feminine third person plural pronouns 'ils' and 'elles'. These are holding spaces accommodating (in)(de)(finite) values, not gender profiles.

The distinction creates a dynamic that disappears in English, where 'ils' and 'elles' both become 'they'. Wanting it back, I-translator found myself adding a subscripted 'm' or 'f', picturing an alternative notation, a poster of the periodic table, on the wall of a classroom, back in 1987. Repurposed unscientifically, but deliberately, here.

Scientific notation shows the instability of an atom; I-translator need a way to flag the instability of a word, of a collective, a plurality, in 2022, in a climate of continuing nuclear threat, and ever-increasing uncertainty.

ruinsruinsruinsruinsruinsruinsruinsruinsruinsruinsruins

_mthey say that _fthey are the missing link that had to break to let their fifteen billion desiring and thinking cells come into being

ofofofofofofofofofofofofofofofofofofofofofofofofofofofof

_mthey seek proof that _fthey exist as all _mthey've found in the road is disposable décor the interchangeable furniture of their homes

thefuturethefuturethefuturethefuturethefuturethefuture

ruinsruinsruinsruinsruinsruinsruinsruinsruinsruinsruinsruinsruins
ofofofofofofofofofofofofofofofofofofofofofofofofofofofofofofofofof
thefuturethefuturethefuturethefuturethefuturethefuturethefuture

 _mthey are the ancestors of the future   with its fossil pictures of their present time   waste ground of their shivers and their moans   hands plunged up to the elbows in tomorrow's excavations   from the blank screens of their urns   to the vacant rectangles of their very own ruins   these are the limits of their mass grave   the script of their *hic et nunc* _mthey stack the lethal shards of their deeds on the roofs of centuries to come   fabricate the archaeological future   their existence has the density of the past in its insolent march of becoming   their monuments grow obsolete in the remembrance of the future   where the hunt for their inscriptions takes place on the printed matter of their stelae   as their names give way to expiry their relevance to the pillory   science rips up their degrees   folklore goes wild for their poems   their modernity switches tone a hundred times

ruinsruinsruinsruinsruinsruinsruinsruinsruinsruinsruinsruinsruins
ofofofofofofofofofofofofofofofofofofofofofofofofofofofofofofofofof
thefuturethefuturethefuturethefuturethefuturethefuturethefuture

ruinsruinsruinsruinsruinsruinsruinsruinsruinsruinsruinsruins

₁they have sorted out the clouds questioned their criminal break-outs
ceased to confuse the depth of the sky with their deep amnesiac desire

ofofofofofofofofofofofofofofofofofofofofofofofofofofofofofofofofofofof

ₘthey flaunt their nuclear arsenals in the soot of the stratosphere mad pyro-
technists at the future's funeral trapezists scaling the cosmic with no net

thefuturethefuturethefuturethefuturethefuturethefuture

ruinsruinsruinsruinsruinsruinsruinsruinsruinsruinsruinsruins
ofofofofofofofofofofofofofofofofofofofofofofofofofofofofofofofof
thefuturethefuturethefuturethefuturethefuturethefuturethefuture

I wouldn't dream of saying that ₘthey all are clowns   some rework
the remains of their fall into despair   set fire to forests to know it all
about nuclear winter   others dress themselves up in a tongue   prefer
to be unaware *frivolity is a violent state*   ₘthey practise death point
blank   like a hologram   their image persisting in the absence of
the mirror   ₜthey seek out the sea-water between the lines   their
force of perpendicular propulsion   sometimes I sleep with the lioness
      moved by the range of her courage   I write to remember a girl
tidied away underground   head studded with huge mountains   in
the cemetery contemporary with twilight   you suddenly become the
visible presence of voice   stop saying that a body can dissolve in
its own tears   wait   *I have almost forgot the taste of fears*

ruinsruinsruinsruinsruinsruinsruinsruinsruinsruinsruinsruins
ofofofofofofofofofofofofofofofofofofofofofofofofofofofofofofofof
thefuturethefuturethefuturethefuturethefuturethefuturethefuture

ruinsruinsruinsruinsruinsruinsruinsruinsruinsruinsruinsruins

ᵢthey know the earth can give way wherever they walk with the scratch of a nail
ᵢthey've deciphered the death-bringing codes the savagery of ways of knowing

ofofofofofofofofofofofofofofofofofofofofofofofofofofofofofofofofofof

ᵢthey've interrupted the sequence erased the in-the-name-of-the-father signature
on bodies blasted off from the zero degree of legend iconoclasts of its darklight

thefuturethefuturethefuturethefuturethefuturethefuturethefuture

ruinsruinsruinsruinsruinsruinsruinsruinsruinsruinsruinsruinsruins
ofofofofofofofofofofofofofofofofofofofofofofofofofofofofofofofofof
thefuturethefuturethefuturethefuturethefuturethefuturethefuture

our visibility is ending   our landscapes are disappearing from the horizon
the earth soaks up our liquids   sweats the blood and the water of our
labour   takes over the networks of our nervous systems   to send new
new generations into orbit   we are the wood of a curious tree   perhaps
the sole survivor of our era   the future settles down into our furnishings
leans its back against our bone vaults   nobody discloses our identity
nor asks to see our letters of credential   nor has any inkling of our
annihilation   our unreadiness for the eclipse   our resistance to giving
up our place   deceit masks up in plain sight   life no longer bides its
time   to make a being corpse   and from the corpse other being   to be
of woman born is no longer such a thing of custom   death has become
anachronistic   the horror of dying archaic   on the tip of the tongue
of an old millennium   comes stumbling   the memory of the future

ruinsruinsruinsruinsruinsruinsruinsruinsruinsruinsruinsruinsruins
ofofofofofofofofofofofofofofofofofofofofofofofofofofofofofofofofof
thefuturethefuturethefuturethefuturethefuturethefuturethefuture

PRIMO SHLLAKU

Translated by Ragip Luta

Primo Shllaku is an Albanian author, born in the northern town of Shkodër in 1947. He only started publishing poetry after the fall of Communism in Albania in the early nineties, because, as he himself says, he was, in principle, against the official socialist realism in literature during the dictatorship. His first volume of poetry, *Flowers of the Night*, came out in 1994. Since then, he has published several other volumes of poetry (*Salty Moon of the Day*; *Words Go to Hell, Too*). Shllaku is also known for his translations into Albanian of Charles Baudelaire, Honoré de Balzac, and Franz Kafka amongst others.

'Castle' is one of Shllaku's more recent poems. As something desirable, 'Castle' here seems to represents some eternal yearning. Hard to achieve, even requiring ruthlessness, it offers the reward of exultation. But that is only ephemeral, since the very next day the 'conqueror' finds oneself 'thrown out in the dust'. The invincibility of the Castle though (high walls, guards on battlements, large gate bolted a thousand times) is matched with the everlasting appetite 'for the umpteenth reconquest'. The novelty that the poem brings in Shllaku's oeuvre is that of a character who does not pride oneself on his fight, but is rather an entity devoid of heroism, a goatskin bag, that continues his permanent struggle towards his aim.

Castle

I conquered it last night
for the umpteenth time
I entered it
I bloodied its walls,
set it ablaze, burnt down,
and went to bed
conqueror.

The following day
I found myself
a goatskin thrown out
in the dust
in front of the large closed gate.
The castle was there
eternal
with high walls
guards on the battlements
like my everlasting appetite
to conquer that castle again.

With the consciousness
of a goatskin bag thrown in the dust
in front of the large gate outside
in front of the gate bolted a thousand times
in front of the high gate with guards on the battlements
as if through fog
I began scheming
for the umpteenth
reconquest.

TOVE DITLEVSEN

Translated by Cynthia Graae and Michael Favala Goldman

Danish author Tove Ditlevsen's penultimate poetry collection, *The Adults* (De Voksne), is a spare, unadorned distillation of her life. Published in 1969, seven years before her suicide, the poems knell this renowned author's lifelong anxiety and pain from childhood's emotional deprivation. In contrast to her earlier, more lyrical collections, these short, stark lines of free verse conceal rhythms and rhymes like neglected children burying dreams. Throughout the collection, Ditlevsen examines conditions breeding neglect. 'Waiting' laments the constriction of motherhood: despite modern progress, in 1969 women still waited for doctors... husbands...unborn children. Today a pandemic keeps mothers at home, balancing employers' demands and children's needs. The poem's reference to 'The man in | the white | gown' evokes current global threats to women's choice.

One by one, the poems in *The Adults* glide to Ditlevsen's devastating conclusion: children are always alone. The last lines of the collection's final poem, 'The Adults 2', are simple and powerful: 'The adults are gone | and will never come home' and in Danish: 'De voksne er gået | og kommer aldrig hjem'.

We two translators, whose backgrounds, ages, and genders might indicate little commonality, worked together to identify with Tove Ditlevsen's anguish and to search for what Cynthia Ozick in 'A Translator's Monologue' might call 'pre-existing' poems. The truth in Ditlevsen's deceptively commonplace language cried out to us both.

Waiting

Despite progress
and new ways of thinking
about many things
women still
spend a lot of
time waiting.

They wait:
for husbands
for children
for quitting time
for workmen
for messengers
for death
and for
the potatoes to boil.

They wait in
maternity clothes
sit in
waiting rooms
get on
waiting lists.

In the waiting room
it is difficult to
occupy the children
they read Donald Duck
and shuffle
their feet.
Behind the door is
the unpredictable
the unruly
the unmanageable
the unforeseen.

The man in
the white
gown
who only does
it once
in a while
maybe something
about odd and
even dates
I must not
mention it directly.

He turns many
away
it costs three
hundred kroner
if he is willing.
I am nauseous
and eat
licorice while
I wait.

Life is
most constricted in the middle
at about
fifty
it expands again
say the grand-
mothers.

Translated by Valzhyna Mort, Ilya Kaminsky and Katie
Farris, Sasha Dugdale and Maddy Pulman-Jones

AL PANTELIAT

Claritas

I am listening to a Chechen refugee
–it's years ago–
speak of bombardments
how she hides under the apartment bldg

for a week
and then in the street she picks up body parts of her neighbours–
in the middle
of my translation class
–it's years ago–

she can't speak hiccups I am trying
to catch meaning
in her tears–
I remember this now, I am crouching in a bomb-shelter
in Kharkiv
with claritas, I remember–
there is no meaning.

(IK/KF)

JULIA CIMAFIEJEVA

Self-portrait as an Avocado Seed

The larger the avocado seed
the sooner it'll sprout

I researched the growing tips
before I stabbed
three toothpicks
into its firm thigh

before I lowered
an ark sealed
hermetically
into a glass of water

by the morning
the shell
     is cracked
the fleshy seed
     split in two

as if two worlds
have come
to a face off

I could call them
here and there
west and east
mine and not mine

and finally
            us and them

one could have

if not for a root
that shoots and grows
between
the two halves

if not for the small head
of a sprout
raised over the water

look:
somebody crawls
out of the ark
in search of a new land

it's me

(VM/HA)

TANYA SKARYNKINA

My Mother Won't Call

I still think
my mother will call
but she didn't take
her mobile phone into death
she did take her wedding ring
a gift from my grandmother
engraved on the inside
with the date
of my grandparents' wedding
I don't remember the exact day
only the year 1928
she also took my shoes
flat shoes
they looked ok in the coffin
my mother only ever wore court shoes
with heels
but they no longer fit her
since she stopped walking
her feet swelled up
but mine looked ok
on her
you could see
she was comfortable in them
although she wasn't coming home
in my shoes anytime
her hand with the wedding ring
would not unlock the door
like lots of others these days
all dying for no reason

there's no time to bury them all separately
and there's no beautiful Ukrainian wake
like my friend said yesterday
about her own grandmother's wake
the tables in a horseshoe
the pies with all their fillings
rice cabbage curds egg
they spent two whole days
in two neighbouring houses
preparing the feast.

The Age of Terrible Skies

No one will have good feelings
about aeroplanes anymore
or helicopters
no one will have good feelings
about them either
or pilots of planes
or pilots of helicopters
it's good that my father was
a land surveyor
and his father
farmed the land
and my great grandfather
and so on
as far back as it goes
in these terrible times
I'm lucky at least in my ancestors.

A Dream Of A Chair in a Field

Café tables
on the grass
as far as the eye can see
tables tables tables
horror grips me
more than when
the only customer
gets up and goes
an upended white chair
lies at the edge of the woods
no one to put it
back on its legs

(SD)

DANA SIDEROS

February

1

This looks like the New Year's holidays
more than anything else.
Everyone is talking about where they're going to go.
There are queues at the shops,
the shelves are swiftly emptying.
My acquaintances are all greeting one another
with the same formula:
Look after yourself – stay strong.
My relatives and friends
are all calling up at the same time.
At night, as you would expect, no one can sleep.
Outside, the sky booms and glitters.

Our gentle beasts
can hardly bear it –
keep further away from the windows,
refuse to go out through the courtyard,
whine at every explosion.
They never liked any of this
even on a real New Year's.
Now even we, surely,
are going to go off it, too.

2

We write to one another, *look after yourself*.
I have already received fifty-two of these messages:
look after yourself.
Fifty-three messages. Fifty-four.
I promise my relatives and loved ones
to look after myself.
I buy non-GMO almond milk
without animal fats
or preservatives.
I wear woollen socks,
smear my hands with cream, drink a lot of water.
I didn't buy
cigarettes
with reduced tar
and charcoal filters.
Because I am looking after myself,
and on the packet it says that smoking kills.
Smoking builds palaces on our cash.
Smoking attacks border outposts.
Smoking sends tanks to a foreign capital.
Smoking came out of the sea,
grew pincers and jaws,
and devours my world –
not just overtly, or shamelessly,
but even deliberately,
licking its lips.
Fifty-seven messages:
look after yourself.
I actually gave up smoking
eight years ago,

when all this started.
But that didn't help.

3
My lungs
decided to attack my heart.
In textbooks this is called,
'an attack in bad faith'.
But this isn't about faith.
Not about faith,
not about relationships,
not about safety.
I simply can't live without my lungs,
or without my heart.
I read some know-it-alls
who write, *oh, come on,*
write that it doesn't hurt, *just a snip and it's done,*
write that you won't even notice,
you'll just have one big lung,
write that there is no heart,
no liver, no kidneys, no stomach.
Soon there will only be a couple of lungs,
breathless,
wretched with covid and tobacco,
and imminent cancer.

24 February 2022, Odesa

(MPJ)

MAŁGORZATA LEBDA

Translated by Elżbieta Wójcik-Leese

The two italicised poems are spoken by Małgorzata Lebda's father – the main protagonist and addressee of *Matecznik / Queen Cells* (2016), an extended elegy and an award-winning life-writing project in verse. Dedicated to soil, the book collects thirty-one poems arranged in four sections, which span a seasonal year in the life of one family and one village: Żelaźnikowa Wielka in the Beskid Mountains of southern Poland, where Lebda grew up. This world – with its fields, forest, apiary and slaughterhouse – is not a mere backdrop to the important figures of father, mother, siblings and villagers, but the book's foundational character. Here animals (bees, cows, dogs, does) and elements (fire and water) contribute to the communal and private rituals of love, illness, healing, death. Thanks to these severe rules guiding and controlling both the village community and its smaller part, family, Lebda's narrator learns life. 'August: holy day ii' is the middle poem in a mini-sequence of harvesting. 'Voices: fragment,' opening the autumnal section, evokes the name of the dead sister, the secret discovered by the living sisters among family papers – the subject of 'magdalena: history of silence' from the second section. Lebda's writing is organic, unflinching yet tender, without the easy nostalgia of someone who has moved away from the countryside but returns to it as a source of strength. Lebda's strength derives not only from her ecological perspective, but also from her body, with its physical hardships and limitations.

august: holy day ii

we are feeding animals with animals i thought
looking at your incomplete teeth and greasy hands

voices: fragment

all my children i dedicated to the earth
i couldn't have done otherwise i remember the day
the pine branch slit open your cheek i thought:
from now on you belong to the forest

i poured propolis on your wound for years observed
the scar heal when the splinter wandered in the vein
towards the heart you asked: death? the first
and last time i heard this word from your mouth

and when i brought home on my skin dark ticks
i saw in your eyes the bottom of a drilled well
with a pocketknife you pulled them out you were
attentive

and when alcohol returned me to the january night
it was you who pulled me from the white i wanted to name
you planetoids call you magdalena

LEONARDO BOIX

Translated by Katrina Naomi

Leo and I met for last autumn in Yorkshire when he was guest reader at an Arvon course at Lumb Bank. In addition to his reading from *Ballad of a Happy Immigrant* (Chatto, 2021), I loved his poetry from an Argentinian Spanish-language collection, *Mar de Noche*, published by Letras del Sur Editora, Buenos Aires, in 2016. I bought a copy and subsequently wrote to Leo to ask if I could translate some of the poems, none of which had previously been translated into English.

I could have translated any of the poems but two, 'Night Swimming' (Leo used the English title in his original version) and 'Medusa' ('Jellyfish'), stood out for me. I have something of an obsession with sea swimming, and chatting over a bottle of Argentinian wine, found that Leo does too. We both swim year-round, and pretty much every day – me in Penzance, Cornwall and Leo in Deal, Kent. In addition, Deal is close to where I grew up, in Margate. I hadn't expected to find poems relating to the Channel of my childhood in *Mar de Noche*. It was wonderful to find these connections with another poet, in addition to a shared passion for languages and of course, poetry.

I sent Leo early drafts of my translations because I'd taken a few liberties with my versions and wanted to ensure he was happy with this. For example, I wanted to keep the rhymes in 'Jellyfish' but occasionally chose to use slant rather than full rhymes to allow a greater sense of flow in English. Leo swiftly and enthusiastically responded to my ideas for keeping the rhymes, rhythms and sense in this way. In the prose poem 'Night Swimming' I also allowed myself a little leeway to make the most of the glorious sense of light in Leo's original.
The process has been one of exchange and ease (thanks Leo!) and I'm delighted that *MPT* is publishing these translations to show another side of Leo's poetry to non-Spanish/Latinx readers.

Night Swimming

The candles have already consumed themselves in the dining room
below, which smelt of supper, of roast lamb with rosemary and burnt
garlic. The bottles of red wine have piled up in the kitchen, along
with the plates on scattered tables. We extinguished the lights in the
house, room by room, left the music playing. Without a word, we
walked Golden Street, slowly crossing Beach Street, which at this
hour was deserted, and went down over the pebbles to the black
beach. In the distance, lights reflected from the Channel. Quivering.
They warned the boats against running aground on the sandbanks.
The restaurant at the end of the pier had already closed; light was
falling. Even the fishermen had gone. We took off our clothes: shirts,
the Bermuda shorts we'd worn all year, sandals. The dark water was
waiting, so much calmer than the Channel. The close night hugged
us. We windmilled our arms, took a deep breath, looked towards
town, lit by orange halogen bulbs, as if for a party. We dunked
ourselves, made for the submerged Goodwin Sands. We listened to
our breath. Put our heads underwater. Black, with night above. We
saw the Big Dipper and Orion's Belt. The sea stilled to a mirror, we
became the current. Night swimming, I said. The moon shone on the
Dover road.

Jellyfish

'Your body must be heard'.
– Héléne Cixious, *The Laugh of the Medusa*.

Dead or alive, suspended
by its tentacles, pulsing
like a plastic bag, the boys
try to trap it: *mind the sting.*

Spit, a mass of mucous
instead of a head, the venous body
utterly transparent
with its vague connections

Fluorescence is its law
a jet of sperm disperses
in the silent current:
millennial medusa

So why
leave you there, drying
in the sun, before this sea
where you no longer belong?

NATASHA KANAPÉ FONTAINE

Translated by Howard Scott

Natasha Kanapé Fontaine is an Innu poet from the community of Pessamit on the North Shore of the St. Lawrence River, who currently lives in Montreal. She is a slam artist, an actor, a visual artist and an activist for Aboriginal and environmental rights. She has published four collections of poetry, *N'entre pas dans mon âme avec tes chaussures, Manifeste Assi, Bleuets et abricots,* and *Nanimissuat Île-tonnerre.* The first three have been translated into English by Howard Scott as *Do not enter my soul in your shoes, Assi Manifesto,* and *Blueberries and Apricots.* She recently also published her first novel, *Nauetakuan.* Natasha Kanapé Fontaine makes extensive use of social media. These two poems originally appeared on Facebook, but the issues they address are ongoing and they are worthy of broader publication.

In the poem 'They will be afraid of us', 'our lost children' refers to the recent revealing of hundreds of unmarked graves of Indigenous children at the sites of former residential schools. 'Our missing women' refers to the hundreds of Indigenous women who have been murdered or gone missing in Canada. In 2015, the federal government established a National Inquiry into Missing and Murdered Indigenous Women and Girls.

They will be afraid of us

they will be afraid of us
now
of our souls
of our ancient spirits
of our lost children
of our missing women

they will fear
now
our drums
our songs of peace
our round dances
our traditions
our cries of reconciliation

our Being-the-world
will be rebuilt
and the animals will run
and the birds will sing
and our children's laughter will ring out

we will become many
we will become strong
we will become dignified
now

and we will bring to the world
the light
to open up the night

and the day
and life
now.

It will be my roots that will dig the earth

It will be my roots that will dig the earth
To draw the water of life
Nothing else
It will be my hair that will cross the earth
To carry the energy of my ancestors
Nothing else
It will be my mouth that will quench its thirst
From the spring of the mountains
And the streams of the fields
And the groundwater
Nothing else
Will drink
From the blood of my legend

I am the direct heir
To all the waters
Where I was born

My crown will be tea plants
And nothing more will burn my forests
When I come back

THE PREVIOUS SONG

Focus on Somali Poetry

Dedicated to Said Jama Hussein

XASAN DAAHIR ISMAACIIL 'WEEDHSAME'

Translated by Martin Orwin

Xasan Daahir Ismaaciil 'Weedhsame' was born in Kalabaydh to the west of Hargeysa in what is now the self-declared Republic of Somaliland. In his early years, he spent time as a refugee in Ethiopia due to the conflict and returned to Somaliland in 1992. After school he went on to study mathematics at the newly opened University of Amoud in Boorame.

He is well known throughout the Somali territories as a versatile and prolific poet. He has written serious poems on social issues and politics such as 'Mudduci' 'Plaintiff' (February 2017) about corruption, which began a long series of poems, the 'Miimley' chain (because they all alliterate in 'm') all on the same theme and to which many young people contributed. He is also very well known for his love poems which are often set to music and sung by famous singers such as Maxamed BK and Ubax Daahir 'Fahmo'.

The poem translated here was written in 2007 and is one he considers his masterpiece in the original sense of the word: a piece to show the master that the apprentice has mastered the craft. Indeed he showed it to his mentor Maxamed Xaashi Dhamac 'Gaarriye' and also to the great Maxamed Ibraahim Warsame 'Hadraawi', who were both very appreciative and acknowledged his reaching a level of mastery in the crafting of poems. It was prompted by seeing a *sogsog* tree in the Xero Awr district of Hargeysa in which there was a species of trailing vine growing (*xayaab* in Somali). He was struck by the beauty of this sight which prompted him to consider how to express beauty in poetry and in particular how to describe a woman in terms which are not specific to an individual. This wonderful work of art displays the features which go towards making a poem of the finest quality: the careful structure, the use of metaphor and imagery, the use of sound, the syntax and its relation to metre, all of which make for a memorable piece which is very much appreciated by audiences when they hear it. I have tried to bring something of the feel of the poem to bear in the translation. It is in the *jiifto* metre, a short line form, and Weedhsame's use in this poem displays his own style in the way the language flows through and across the lines, a characteristic I have tried to bring out in particular.

This is a very slightly amended version of a translation first published in: Orwin, Martin. 2020. 'Crafting Modern Somali Poetry: Lyric Features in "Fad Galbeed" by Gaarriye and "Xabagbarsheed" by Weedhsame'. *Journal of African Languages and Literatures* 1: 110–40. https://doi.org/10.6092/JALALIT.V1I1.6737.

Royal Jelly

O lightning-flash rain
O scarlet sash of dawn
O Dagaari nebula
frill of its shawl.

O sunset cirrus
the rain-promise bloom
swathes, dyed
blood-red above.

O risen rainbow
whose scarf lifts
revealing stripe
by stripe the spectrum's
silky sweep of colour.

O hennaed moon
haloed by a mist-
soft glow, the veil
is shed and you free
a darkened corner
of the world with light.

O tree in blossom,
the cloudburst cleansed
last night its branches,
the foaming flood
cleared the dust,

and fresh-water lappings
tended its roots;
now leaves and petals
vie and tussle,
across their bounds;
while verdure and shoots
take up the moisture
at waist and elbow
and sweep its trunk,
the spine of the sun
and its chest emit
acute-angle rays
of light it urges
through the breaking day.

You're a chestnut mare
who hasn't heard
the call to the camel raid
the quarters of conflict;
hasn't suffered the dry
drought-laden land
nor dregs of pasture;
she's cared for and grazes
at night in the bush
where the pond sits
and dew crouches
among the grass;
never hurt by a whip
nor touched by a stick,
her downy fur smoothes
over her ribs and limbs;

fenced-off in her hollow,
people arrive to view
the filly at home
their eyes turn gently
like white spring flowers
toward her striking form:
you are more beautiful
than the houris by far.
Like the arteries that carry
the blood to the depths
of the body, you, a star,
reached the core of my soul;
you're the proof of love;
my whole being wishes
you become my wife.

What sowed the desire
the yearning in me?
Your virtue, patience,
knowledge, modesty,
the conscientious
respectful nature
God has placed in you.
You are the truth;
with friends and family
you show the highest
virtues of women.
Free from caprice,
O navel of eloquence:
like spinning a rope
you tie together

wisdom and metaphor,
the choicest words
that soothe the mind,
you excel in composing
the sweetness of speech.

O royal jelly!
When we met, I
etched you in my chest;
I kept it secret,
hidden, held tight;
now longing has broken
the burden of concealing
and waves of desire
have brought me to shore:
Hayaad, this evening
for a home and passion
shall we prepare the ground?

ASMAA JAMA

In my work, I'm interested in the coast or sea as a site for myths and stories, and the ways me and my family have interacted with the ocean. In this poem, I was inspired by a fragment of a song my father would sing when I was younger, about the ocean, whether there was any shadow or respite there. Growing up, my father would translate songs and gabays, and I now find the work I write and the work I gravitate towards is often melodic and alliterative because of these worlds. Although my own attempts to write in the gabay form failed, I find it interesting to not replicate it, but shift and refract it.
A lot of my access to this world is through this lens. I am always mistranslating, mishearing, misunderstanding. In this poem, I tried and failed at finding the original song and instead found myself writing this.

Baddaan badan hoos ma leedahay

maryan sang, my shadow, in all this water, who owns my name
my father pulled us away from the coastline, until our limbs bloated
and we were afraid, so we used the tide like it was a tether, and we came
    back sand-filled i'm sure the sea is exhausted of me mentioning its
    name, and never writing any elegies sea, who folds in its mouth the
    teeming everyone made to cross water
and wasn't it my grandfather, who sat in his house, its corrugated tin roofs,
    away from water, sat inside, when it rained, let the camels' fur grow
    damp, let them come in droves looking for shelter
and in nairobi, didn't my grandmother, hold our mouths open to water, as
    if it was the sea, being cut out of the air, and didn't we bleach our
    sheets white fill our scars, call it salt and a blessing
the sea, is already thirty five parts salt, could not consume us even if it
    wanted to, my father whispered, and held our fingers and told us float
and they all knew how to swim, or they said that they did, said they were
    always at the mouth, at the coastline, and they went in arms raised
and my uncle, was the only one, who knew how to collect fish, strew their
    mouths open, and make them small fruitful dawns,
i mean my uncle was a boat, freshly carved, beautiful in water,
i mean my uncle was forever dappled and damp, on land, he sat with his
    palms, to his ocular bone, held it closed, and it kept leaking, and i
    could never tell if it was because of me, or the tear gas
my uncle a moored boat, landlocked lies in a shallow bath, of water, he
    keeps telling us, he can chart the globe, he keeps telling us that the
    night is clear
he can flatten the sea, like a bedsheet and we ask him to stay,
whole in nairobi, say we have no more flames, can do no more ceremonies
    for the gone, and he does, wood turning soft, soft body in decay

HIBAQ OSMAN

'In Order of Relevance' was inspired by Somali poet Hawa Jibril (1920–2011) who was a 12-year-old nomadic girl when she composed and recited her first poem, after a family squabble. For the rest of her life her poetry challenged colonialism and women's oppression. 'Waa ii gunuunucahayaa' or 'Why he is grumbling' (1932), is one of her more famous poems, and documents a family fight wherein a daughter in the family eats from the male side of the dish. In my poem, I wanted to play with this idea in a modern setting where new rules apply.

In Order of Relevance

We do not sit at a table together,
dishing meats and fluffy grains

When the youngest leans over stove-top
we pause, and let her take

With each passing second
we have a world between us

Withered with miles and age,
wet tongues fake a silence

In badaan soo gur
whispered directly into her stomach

Where our youngest goes
we'll follow, antidote to loneliness

When she eats, so then will we,
with enough to go around twice

AMRAN MAXAMED AXMED

Translated by Said Jama Hussein and Anna Selby

On the 6th of August 1992, Amran Mohamed Ahmed was invited
to the City Hall in Helsinki for a remembrance event for Hiroshima.
August 6th is the day when in 1945, the United States dropped the
world's first deployed atomic bomb. Three days later, they dropped
another on Nagasaki. Amran subsequently wrote this poem to
contribute to a memorial for Hiroshima. It encapsulates the
ongoing cruelty, futility, and devastation of this and so many wars
and conflicts.

Amran is a prominent author, educator, and activist, particularly
in Scandinavia and the UK, as well as Somaliland and Somalia; and
has been a driver in championing women's literature. In 2001, she
co-edited a tri-lingual anthology, in which she collected 60 pieces
of orature from Somali women living in Finland. Amran once said
at a conference: 'If we look at Somali women from a historical
perspective, we find they have always been composing poetry... But
because of the lack of encouragement from society, meaning mainly
from men, women have not been able to raise their voices loudly
until the end of the 20th century'.

Buraanbur is a centuries-old, female Somali poetic form. In the
mid-20th century, well-known female poets, activists and anti-
colonialists like Timiro Ukash, Xawa Tako and Halima Godane
began to use this form to address the fight for independence from
Britain and Italy, joining the fight with the force of their voices and
continuing to compose poetry when they were imprisoned. Growing
on this tradition, Amran created the *guubaabo*, a poem composed by
women to give advice and encouragement, calling attention to the
difficulties and dangers of a situation, and urging the listener, and
reader, to do their best to overcome it. In Amran's poetry, she holds
true to the role of poet as social conscience and agitator.

Amran writes and publishes poetry and journalism in Finnish and Somali, lives in London, and was born in Somaliland's capital and largest city, Hargeisa, in 1954. Her father worked for the British army. In 1990, she moved to Finland, dedicating much of her time to educating people on Somali culture and supporting Somali refugees fleeing the civil war after the fall of Siad Barre and the bombing of Hargeisa. She worked as a volunteer interpreter and advocated for the rights of refugees, especially women and children. In 2005, the Finnish Refugee Council named her 'Woman of the Year' and six years later her biography was published, *In Search of Peace*.

'The Killing Ground' was translated with Somali translator and scholar, Said Jama Hussein, for *So At One With You*, a dual-language anthology, co-published by the Poetry Translation Centre, Kayd and Redsea Online. Within the poem, some of Amran's life's work and experiences rise up to us in rebuke, and lead to a concentration and truth of emotion that thrashes.

The Killing Ground

After all their bloodied years
Of bloodied acts, the murderers'
Blood-coloured hands
Were witnessed
By us everywhere
Next to, under, atop us
When Iblis' flash
Lashed, loosed
Every day began
With a new victory
Praised, shouted across
A wasted land

On how many killing grounds
Have perfect houses
Been struck
Shattered, dashed

How many children
Left, lost
Found themselves
One day, scattered

How many people could be seen
Walking emptied streets
Senseless
Directionless

How many have we seen
Crawl, their stumps
Dragging, their limbs
Slashed

How many have left their homes
Fled to unknown towns
To become unwelcomed
In unpronounceable countries

If we could say that bullets
Are a whistle of success
Africa would be a champion
Every dusk they're sprayed
Thousands of bodies
Roll into pits

Without compassion
Void of understanding
One afternoon
Hiroshima was burnt away
Each year
That day repeats itself
Striking in our memory
An August silence

The truth is
What we do wrong
Will be brought back
On us

Houses wrecked
Animals struck
For what?
Even the birds
Vault from the trees
Abandoning the fruit
To fall
Hoping skies
Will offer shelter

These men, beginning
And beginning again
New civil wars, new conflicts
Will they ever get tired
Will they never stop?

If we can't stop them
Pressing lit matches to gas
Then what? At home
We lie awake in our beds
Should we be done then
With our planet, head out
To Mars, or beyond that
Waving a white banner
To a darkening sky?

ALI OSMAN DROG

Translated by Ayan Salaad

'Hooyaalaadee', a Banaadiri hees hawleed (work song) composed by
Ali Osman Drog, is traditionally performed by women while they
spin, sew and weave. Ali Osman Drog was a distinguished Banaadiri
abwaan (wiseman) who was famous for composing many poems.
When it came to heeso (songs), in particular, he tended to compose
the words or lyrics of heesaha dhaqanka ee Banaadiriga (Banaadiri
cultural songs), heesaha ammaanta (praise songs), and heesaha
jacaylka (love songs).

'Hooyaalaadee' was made famous by the renowned singer Faduma
Qasim Hilowle when she performed it on Somali Television in the
1980s. Faduma Qasim Hilowle was a revered Somali singer and was
given the nickname 'Feynuuska Fanka', which roughly translates
as 'the lantern of the arts', not only to signify her substantial
contribution to Somali arts and culture but also to highlight how she
lit the way for many other artists and entertainers who came after
her. Faduma was famous for singing a range of heeso, which included
heesaha waddaniga (nationalist songs), heesaha dhaqanka (cultural
songs), heesaha ammaanta (praise songs), and heesaha jacaylka
(love songs).

The second translation is of 'Waa Guuriheeynnaa' (We are taking
her to the marital home), a hees (song) composed by the abwaan
Ali Osman Drog to celebrate and preserve traditional female
Banaadiri wedding customs both within the Banaadiri community
and wider Somalia. It is regularly performed during the female-only
Banaadiri wedding tradition called the meel fadhiisis. It was also
made famous when Faduma Qasim Hilowle performed it on Somali
television in the 1980s.

The renditions of these songs are translated from performances
by Faduma Qasim Hilowle's daughter, Aisha Karama Saed, in her

home in London. As Aisha was born into a family of singers and musicians, she was involved in Banaadiri culture and music from a young age. She would sing in the chorus of her mother's performances from the age of seven and was given an even greater role in supporting her mother's work as she grew older.

Hooyaalaadee

The previous song.

The previous song.

It is the previous song. I am not forgetting it.

The man who has his work finds a livelihood.

The man who has his work finds a livelihood.

He finds a livelihood.

Sleep is not better for us. We have slowly walked from it.

Sleep is not better for us. We have slowly walked from it.

Weave the mat for me and the basket.

Weave the mat for me and the basket.

And the basket.

It is the character of our country. We are not tiring from it.

It is the character of our country. We are not tiring from it.

I am adding to the sewing of a hat.

I am adding to the sewing of a hat.

I am sewing.

I am making it sufficient for every person to have his allotted role.

I am making it sufficient for every person to have his allotted role.

I am propagating it. I make a reputation for it.

I am propagating it. I make a reputation for it.

I honour it.

I am propagating the flat bread grinding stone.

Mixing the item one wants with it.

The spinning wheel and this thread.

The spinning wheel and this thread.

And this thread.

Embroidering the cloth one wants with it.

Embroidering the cloth one wants with it.

It is the previous song. I am not forgetting it.

It is the previous song. I am not forgetting it.

It is the previous song. I am not forgetting it

Waa Guuriheeynnaa

A maiden and a previously married woman,
those of us who have attended this meeting
have affection for the bride.
We are taking her to the marital home.

We have affection for the bride.
We are taking her to the marital home.

A maiden and a previously married woman,
those who have attended this meeting,
have affection for the bride.
We are taking her to the marital home.

We have affection for the bride.
We are taking her to the marital home.

The glowing skin,
this reddish brown and layered dappled design,
these girls at the meeting place,
put it on with their hand.

These girls at the meeting place,
put it on with their hand.

The glowing skin,
this reddish-brown and layered dappled design,
these girls at the meeting place,
put it on with their hand.

These girls at the meeting place,
put it on with their hand.

Guineas that are gold
were put on her ankles until the neck for her.
She achieved it.
God supported her with it.

She achieved it.
God supported her with it.

Guineas that are gold
were put on her ankles until the neck for her.
She achieved it.
God supported her with it.

She achieved it.
God supported her with it.

This knotted cloth,
This silk shawl on top of the shoulder,
It is the law that is previous.
We do not divert from it.

It is the law that is previous.
We do not divert from it.

This knotted cloth,
This silk shawl on top of the shoulder,
It is the law that is previous.
We do not divert from it.

It is the law that is previous.
We do not divert from it.

We have affection for the bride.
We are taking her to the marital home.

We have affection for the bride.
We are taking her to the marital home.

LIKE HONEY:
AN INTRODUCTION TO SOMALI POETRY

By Ibrahim Hirsi

It is sometime in the 19th century. Under a Galool tree, a group of community elders have formed. They've come together for a serious issue: their traditional leader has been overstepping his boundaries and abusing his position. In an egalitarian society such as the one of the Somali nomads this is unthinkable. And so these elders choose five poets of the highest calibre and summon the Ugaas (Sultan). The five poets stand up, one by one and recite poems they've composed, with striking imagery, veiled warnings and strong arguments, and the Ugaas is shamed into abdicating his throne.

Such is the power of Somali poetry, far from being a benign art form appreciated only by a few, and seen as being the domain of the wealthy and artistic, it is an empowered device. Maybe this is why poetry has been of such fascination to the myriad of scholars who have travelled to the Horn of Africa over the past 200 years.

Up until very recently Somali society was mainly an oral one. Histories, traditional stories and indigenous knowledge were all passed down via the tongue. Somali poetry is governed by rules of alliteration and metre making it easy to memorise and therefore pass down. It's through this culture of composition and dissemination that traditions and history have been preserved.

Poetry or 'Maanso' in its widest definition is like honey. There are hundreds of different forms of poetry practised by the Somalis. Liquid enough to fill the spaces it is poured into but sticky enough to leave a mark on whatever it leaves. The lullabies full of admiration and prayer a mother sings to her newborn; the songs nomads chant to their camels, placating them during a long and tiring journey, and the metrically complicated Gabay used for scathing political and social critique all come under the remit of the Maanso.

As mass urbanisation and social change was occurring during the mid-20th Century, many of these varied forms of poetry that were differentiated by metre, function and occasion had begun to fall out of common use and were in danger of disappearing. The Gabay has long been considered the highest form of art. Along with the Geeraar and Masafo, it had been considered one of the few poetic genres adept for 'weighty' topics, i.e handling socio-political and economic issues. Thus they were the domain of the traditional intellectuals. As a result, use of these genres for things seen as being 'lesser' issues, such as love, were held as sacrilegious. In fact, when a popular youth movement known as Qaraami erupted in Somaliland during the 30s, many of the older generation at the time saw it as defiling the Gabay form. The reason being this was a poetry movement completely dedicated to love and their choice of form was the Gabay.

However, during the late 60s a new tide had begun, whereby the Gabay was slowly being phased out in terms of popularity. These were the years of the Jiifto, a short line form that was traditionally used as an accompaniment to dance. A major part of this movement was the Lafoole School of Poetry, a group of modern poets/intellectuals who had worked on *Aqoon iyo Afgarad*, a famous play, together. Including Sa'eed Saleh, Gaarriye, and Hadraawi, this group nearly exclusively worked with 'lesser' forms such as the Jiifto. Soon forms such as Maroodi Cadhoole, a children's play song, were being used for political philosophy and to discuss social issues. As a result many poetic genres that were dying out became revitalised. This shift allowed for the development of Somali poetry, letting it grow and become more textured and made room for more experiments. The popularity of short forms was cemented by the Siinley chain of poetry in 1973, as it was nearly entirely carried out with Jiiftos, firmly positioning this form as popular and important.

Poetry chains in Somalia are a type of communal debate.

A disgruntled poet would compose a controversial piece and soon dozens of poets would send their replies to the poem and then other poets would send their replies to the original replies and so on and so on, creating a web of poetry all centred around a specific issue. Chains of poetry are important because they give us a layered view on how early Somali communities viewed specific issues. Rather than just having a single poem on a certain issue, we'd have dozens, agreeing and disagreeing with each other giving us a more nuanced and layered view on the public opinion of certain issues. Some of the most famous chains have touched on nationalisms, love, women's rights, areas of contention in theology, etc.

I've long considered poetry as a living, breathing, tangible part of Somali life. In each family, it is not rare to find a casual poet. History and folklore have proved its power as a social force. It serves as a site of debate, preservation, change and most importantly for me, Somali poetry acts as witness. As the famous proverb says: 'A poet may pass away but their poetry will remain'.

ASHA JAMA DIRIYE

Translated by Ibrahim Hirsi

Asha Jama Diriye was a singer, poet and actress. Born in 1940 in
El-Afweyn, Asha spent her formative years between Hargeisa,
Berbera and Erigavo. Asha moved to Djibouti where she would
end up settling down and getting married. Asha passed away in
2004 in Djibouti.

Composed by Asha Jama Dirie in 1972, this poem was part of the
Siinley poetry chain. Asha created this poem in the voice of the
principal character of this chain, 'Saharla' (lit. speckless/perfect).
Saharla embodies Djibouti, at that time still under French
colonialism – the poetry chain was a debate on how she would fit
under a 'Greater Somalia', a nationalistic dream that shaped much
of the literature from this period. Full of allegory and riddles, this
poem was one of the last ones in the chain. Due to Djibouti
(Asha/'Saharla') having spoken for herself, many of the previous
poets who contributed to the chain could no longer say they
conversed with her and knew her wishes and wants and so could
not argue on her behalf.

When giving this poem to Hadraawi (the starter of this chain)
Asha accompanied with it a sword, a folded toga and the flag of
Somalia. The cassette upon which the poem was recorded also
contained a short play Asha authored. News of these gifts and
speculations of what they could mean spread like wildfire, even
reaching the president.

As a result the items were confiscated, and soon afterward
Hadraawi was imprisoned.

We are at Peace this Morning

By prayers of peace, the verses of Yaasiin and the great chapters
To all those who live in Lafoole, I send you my greetings.
Wherever a person's belongings lie are where they must stay
And whoever finds this part of me will be amongst you
So as you are now, complete, I journey to you.
Those who have waited for my news; live long and in peace
And the one who said in his poem 'I am coming', do not pass me by
O My kin, O Samaale, O the Good, O you who are made within me.
O Kind Maxamed, Abu Hadra and Samatar, listen to me
Raise your voices, my loved ones, and let them know of Saharla's situation
To your leaders transmit this chanted poem, surely it is a crucial one

I have imprinted those verses with 'S' and now I move onto another.
As a Somali and one who will not accept vague words,
Whose name is Saharla I move onto another

And so accept this sword for I wish for us to be well
And take this folded toga that I have placed with it.
They are probing us due to the three Fridays I visited you,
Sa'eed Saalah is a witness of this
So wear the sword against these men who would contaminate us
And don't be idle from responsibility, a real man fights deeply.

To God the emaciated
and those who reside by wells are equal
To God a shackled man
and the one who walks freely are equal
To God a man who has lost his wealth
and the one who amply milks she-camels are equal

And so to God, a man who is held by love and one who still waits
    for it are equal

I have imprinted those verses with 'S' and now I move onto another.

In some things men are equal
One is the trio of weapons they carry,
One is their blood price,
However if hard times and the heat of war ensue,
Where 'turn back' and 'retreat' are cried and dust flies upwards,
One who has thrown ten weapons and the one who flees cannot be
    treated the same.
These men who have elaborated on Saharla and her condition
I will likewise differentiate them for they deserve different things
I will not delve deeper and say who they are, however I will say
That they are our relatives and people with whom we share a mark
And I shall give you all that which you are owed
There are three riddles
Answer them well for I wish not for you to fail

1. A man your perfect mother has given birth to, with whom you
    slept in the same womb
Who you've eaten maize with and know deeply
Yet is not your brother under any circumstance

2. A rain eagerly awaited for that has not come when expected

3. A sultanate of camels and a she-camel who's given birth that
    travels with them

I have imprinted those verses with 'S' and now I move onto another.

Those who said 'we met with Saharla and stayed till morning'
They did not see her at all, these men are just ranting
They've seen a false image or maybe the devil
He who said Saharla is a lie come out into the day
And the man who sows conflict between me and my husband
Know that we are at peace this morning

RAAGE UGAAS WARFAA

Translated by Martin Orwin

We don't know the dates of Raage Ugaas Warfaa, though he certainly lived during the nineteenth century and ca. 1810 and ca. 1840 have been given in different sources for his birth. He is, however, one of the most important poets in the history of Somali poetry. His poems are some of the earliest we know, having been passed from one generation to the next before being written down only later in the second half of the twentieth century. He is said by some to be the finest of all Somali poets, and I would suggest it is because they are such wonderfully vivid and aesthetically rich poems that still speak to us today that they have been remembered over and over.

Raage was the son of an ugaas, a lineage leader, and stories of his life have also been passed down. He is known as well-educated in religion, and skilled in peacefully handling disputes in the nomadic pastoralist society in which he lived. His poems are in both gabay and geeraar forms, which continue to be used today. All poetry in Somali is metrical and alliterative with the same consonant sound being sustained throughout the poem. The gabay is a long line form comprising two half-lines, each of which includes an alliterating word. The geeraar on the other hand is a short line form with an interesting metrical pattern. The geeraar is considered to be a form made to be recited on horseback, though the form also appears in other contexts and today is used for various topics.

This poem is in praise of the poet's horse, Walhad. Raage uses 'w', from the name of the horse, as the alliterating sound. 'W' is one of the more challenging sounds to use for alliteration and the adept way he weaves the alliterating words in the lines such that they come across naturally is testament to his skill. At the beginning of some sections of the poem he uses alliterating epithets which I have kept in the translation along with some hint as to their meaning.

The geeraar form has its own feel with respect the flow of language, as all metrical patterns do. Not all lines are of the same length and we often hear grammatical function words which are extrametrical, that is which don't form part of the actual metrical line. In the translation I have tried to present something of this by including function words at the end of some lines, in particular conjunctions and prepositions.

Walhad

Where one man makes a *geeraar* well
another's confined in its ravine:
it's a man like me who knows
the news, the promise that it brings.

O Walhad! My stallion!
I've praised you in these words
they're few, do I begin,
do I alliterate with 'w'?
The measure of a horse
is marked in different ways.

O Weehad! In gallop he flies.
Is he a stone that's flung from a sling
fast down a gorge, is he
a telegram sent through a wire?
When reined with skill does he
keep to the course in the open?

O Wayrah! Defender – his nature
when taken to water is such that if
before he's quenched his thirst and
I am not by his side, then
in easy fury he'll kill
the man who drives him from
the well and others nearby.
Is he a wild rhinoceros?

O Weedhaan! Fast swerver!
In speed is he a wandering lion that
takes a goat as prey and when
he hears 'Shoo!' from people who
would chase him away – turns,
leaps and pounces upon them?

Weris! His colour is
the cloudless drying sky when
the chill and damp of night is gone;
the plumage of the ostrich chick
before it's white; is he
the tint of dawn that crimsons?

In battle drawn, where enemies
with lances pierce each other, there
I mend my heart through him,
a son that God has given you;
is he my brother, true?

When he's facing what's my due and
is chasing something down with me
is he the paths that flow
with pelting rain to wells; is he
a river-bed in spate?

If I say 'Turn away!' from
the rope that ties his legs
he sets himself in frenzy free
he flings his head and from his eyes
his look is manic; is he
a sorcerer who knows?
Magic that foretells?

He saves me from the limb-slicing
spear and spares me from
the javelin tipped with bane,
from arrow-heads that glint
from the rounds of bullets shot.

Is he a famous scholar of
religion who has always known
the virtue of the Forty Hadith who,
when a ram is slaughtered, will
recite for you the two
suras: The Night, and then
The Morning Light?

When all the people sleep if
I release him from the fold and
tether him, he waits,
without defiance, now,
with womanly good, is he
the one who spreads a mat
for you to sleep at night,
attentive to advice you give,
accepting of your counsel?

THIRTY-ONE QARAAMI VERSES

Translated by WN Herbert and Said Jama Hussein

Qaraami is the popular music of Somali culture dating from the 1940s, embodied in the marriage between the intense love poetry of its lyrics and the rich musical heritage of the Red Sea area, led instrumentally by the oud then, in the cultural renaissance of the 1970s, reframed in an Afrobeat style. As a cultural event it might be compared to London in the 'swinging' sixties, the marriage between bebop and beat in the US in the 1940s and 50s, and indeed the post-war Rembetika movement in Greek culture. Passion in its most intense form is at its core, and the brief verses translated here formed the basis of impassioned performances, many of which were recorded and preserved in the archive of Radio Hargeisa through the years of conflict which followed. Now they are being recovered, digitised, and revisited by musicians old and new. The verses are by turns teasing, pithy, metaphysical, persuasive, full-throated, and desperate – in both the performative and the heartrendingly genuine senses. As determining their authorship is a complex matter, they are presented here without ascription.

Thirty-One Qaraami Verses

1

Misery marks my days
insomnia haunts my nights –
please mend this mangled life.

2

How nice if you'd note my news
and credit my account.

3

Long life and no pleasure
makes hoping hapless.

4

When is your trial due
and can I be judge?

5

This is not my right mind
when she went it left too.

6

You so battered my heart's arteries
you cannot be survived.

7

One tree in all the town, my dear,
whose tone takes after you.

8

The thirsty man wants water –
what's lacking, then, for us?

9

Since fate and fortune fix it so
you're lost to me, at least live well.

10

God's grace in her every part
and perfect particle – no complaints from me.

11

If they'll never let me have her to myself
what good will waiting do me?

12

Since my praise could leave no doubt
it's your turn, Haybe – I'm listening.

13

Broken stones won't keep up houses
so too with my cheekbones' glow.

14

Staggering beneath this lovesickness
I'm too languid for its load.

15

Denied the drug that heals me
banished by uncaring kin
women look at me askance
and for its contrary choice
mock my moping heart.

16

A man can lie down in his grave
but this love's neither here nor there.

17

Onward with my heavy freight
tottering from foot to foot
wondering what eats me up.

18

I jitter about all night
but can't lift my feet by day –
did I fall out with the sun?

19

Like a wolf in the wild I won't go to sleep
and pass the night with one eye open.

20

I kept my wound beneath a blanket for so long
that everybody knew it wouldn't heal.

21

Your death is God's decision
anything less is my concern.

22

It's because I haven't seen her for an age
that my heart keeps leaping up like this.

23

Honey, since I've been hanging round a while,
how high have I climbed in your regard?

24

I'm haunted nightly in my room
by a photo of my sweet Sayida.

25

Your love is too heavy for me
like wearing a necklace of steel

26

Since the Qaraami moves her so
let's try another chorus.

27

When passion's blows pelt down
I won't deny it pains me.

28

The clouds that thunder at dawn
bring this refreshing scented breeze.

29

If the way you treat me won't cure me
God has not written that I should get well.

30

Let's say you're a flower – a fragrant one –
then you would have the sweetest scent.

31

Night worries keep me awake
when will you share their load?

Trap, Comb, Scaffold, Horse

John Clegg reviews *The Lascaux Notebooks* by Jean-Luc Champerret, trans. Philip Terry, Carcanet, 2022.

The Lascaux cave-paintings were made about 12000 years before Stonehenge, and as everyone knows are almost frighteningly vivid; even to scroll through them on a laptop screen is to feel a genuine connection with real Upper Paleolithic individuals, to feel that (in the words of John Berger) humanity had 'grace from the start'. The people who made the paintings certainly had a tradition of poetry, a human universal found in every society documented so far. What Philip Terry's magnificent, mischievous book posits or imagines is that they also had a tradition of *written* poetry, and that this tradition is recoverable.

In the book's framing narrative, Terry discovers a cache of papers left by the poet and amateur paleontologist Jean-Luc Champerret, in which Champerret, who had surveyed the caves in the 1940s as a possible hideout for the French Resistance, becomes obsessed with various repeating signs among the cave-paintings, interpreting them not as decoration but as pictograms. Another little-remarked-on element of the Lascaux artwork are 'the curious, but frequent, three by three grids of squares that decorate the walls of the cave, most notably in the polychrome blazon below the Black Cow in the Nave of Lascaux'. This becomes the jumping-off point for Champerret's astonishing Oulippean project: placing the 'pictograms' in the squares, to produce nine pictograms over three lines, and then translating the resulting poems.

The translations begin as glyph-by-glyph paraphrases:

			eye	night	flute
			night	star	star
			bird call	night	trees

Then, over various interim versions, we watch the poem develop via the mediation of the translator, until:

> Being sleepless at
>   midnight I rise
>   to play my flute
>
> The clear night sky
>   is filled with a thousand
>   stars gazing at me
>
> A lonely bird
>   calls out in darkness
>   from the heart of the wood

Paradoxically, this text at four removes – a translation which is necessarily highly interpretative, of a procedurally generated poem, recorded in the notebooks of the mysterious 'Champerret' and then rendered into English via Terry – allows enough imaginative distance for the final effect to be entirely believable. The final translations often record hesitancies, [?]s, alternate readings; the reader, who has watched the poem being built up, participates with the translator, and the final voice (Alice Oswald describes it as 'the Spiritual Exercises of a Paleolithic Loyola') is a co-creation.

Nine-line lyric poems of this sort, sometimes ratcheted a further step into a Mallarméan visual poem sprawling across two pages, make up Champerret's 'Carnet Noire', his first notebook of Lascaux translations; in the 'Carnet Bleu', the 'Carnet Gris', and a further selection of poems on loose paper, Champerret experimented with different grid-sizes and strategies of interpretation. For these longer poems, Terry omits the interim stages, which by this point the reader can take on trust. What emerges is remarkable, a generative Ice Age mythology, with its own creation stories, hero narratives, a war between black bulls and red horses (a Lascaux cave-painting come to life). A few of these are expanded convincingly into sustained prose narratives.

So far, Champerret had read his grids left-to-right and top-to-bottom; in the 'Carnet Gris' he tries different permutations, rendering the same poem in different versions read right-to-left, bottom-to-top etc. Here if anywhere I would have expected the generative process to feel like an obstacle, an out-of-place Oulippean artificiality; instead I found them the most vivid and moving poems in the book. The sequences are too long to quote in full, but here are the first and last renderings through different text-directions of the fourth poem in the Carnet Gris:

a)
The sound of birds | at night | fills out ears | or is it that in the forest | hunters imitate their calls | in the night | the hair left | in the comb | a woman's

[...]

d)

The sleeping woman | at night | hears nothing | comb hunters |
come out | after dark | the hair | a forest | without birds

Again, I'm amazed that a generative process can produce something
with the eerie inexorability of genuine folklore; these lines, and the
other poems in this section, remind me of nothing so much as the
Serbian songs and spells collected by Vasko Popa and translated by
Anne Pennington as *The Golden Apple*.

Occasionally, behind this entirely achieved folkloric anonymity,
we glimpse moments of playfulness on behalf of the translators.
Putting the same sign in all nine positions in the grid produces, early
on, some surprisingly convincing poems, but near the end ('reindeer
reindeer reindeer | reindeer reindeer reindeer | reindeer reindeer
reindeer') one joyously silly one; and the final poem in the book,
arrived at through the grid-system quite plausibly, is too good not
to quote in full:

So much depends
upon the red bison
from the hills

Their pelts glazed
with rain water
in the evening sun

Surrounded by
the white birds
of the air

We have been given one final untranslated grid, on the book's cover: it replicates the sign translated by Champerret as 'watchman, eyes, happiness, horse', and the sign translated as 'trap, comb, scaffold, horse'. Taking the 'horse' as metonymic for inspiration, and noting that the second pictogram's 'scaffold' seems to itself represent a set of grids – therefore, 'inspiration [/attention] trapped in grid form' – I would translate the two signs together as the Paleolithic equivalent of *Collected Poems*.

Women, War, and Translation as Weapon

Sana Goyal reviews *Leaving* by Anar, translated by Hari Rajaledchumy with Fran Lock, Poetry Translation Centre, 2021, and *Euripides' The Trojan Women: A Comic,* by Rosanna Bruno and Anne Carson, Bloodaxe, 2021.

The act – and art – of translation is dual: a closing in and an opening out. Depending on where you stand, where you're looking from, translation brings you closer to something specific – another language, another way of life – whilst opening and broadening that specificity unto the world. It's a simultaneous zooming in *and* zooming out. Responsibility, fidelity and fluency are three words that often form epithets to the politics and ethics of translation as praxis, while the notion of a source language and a target language misleadingly implies that the process is unidirectional, linear, arguably even passive.

If Anar's *Leaving* – a bilingual pocket-sized selection from the poet's five award-winning collections – offers English-language readers an introduction to one of Sri Lanka's most treasured Tamil poets, via translators Hari Rajaledchumy and Fran Lock (and an afterword from Vidyan Ravinthiran), then poet and classicist Anne Carson's *Euripides' The Trojan Women: A Comic* offers a re-introduction to the ancient Greek epic in a graphic comic format through visual artist Rosanna Bruno's black-and-white illustrations. Through these two acts of translation, two sets of tales and tragedies are given new life and new form – speaking centuries of silence – through the state, through stories – into existence in the current era. Through daring acts of dissent, creativity and liberty with the text – and with received ideas of poetry and translatability – these translators and artists, through their interventions and meandering imaginations, offer works that are phantasmagoric and eccentric, rebellious and ambitious, irreverent and elegant.

In Rajaledchumy's introduction to *Leaving*, she writes that in the original Tamil, Anar's 'short lines care little for grammatical boundaries and sequential logic'; the 'end-stopped lines often bleed into each other, sometimes with elliptical pauses'. The result surprises the reader, ricochets them into dream-like circulations and free-associations, she notes. Rajaledchumy and Lock chose not to retain this in their rendering of the poems in translation; instead, the duo introduced punctuation and reworked lineation. Such elements of Anar's poetics were 'difficult to replicate faithfully in the English translation and diluted the urgency of the voice', she admits. And yet, this 'unfaithfulness' is not a loss. Reading Anar's thirteen poems, one realises that the power of her poetics lies within that which is unexpected and unsaid, or implied – in the free-fall of unknowing.

In 'Further Additional Blood Notes', she writes:

Though used to seeing blood every month,
I am still shaken when a child
comes to me bawling with a cut finger.

The poet often makes such surprising and swift movements from the body personal to the body political, showing how the two are inextricably intertwined in her daily reality. As the poem goes on, the body of a specific child shifts to the omnipresent scene of a battlefield ('blood congeals on crazed streets'). Through another poem, 'Raindrops on a Cashew Tree' – an elegy for Chandrabose Suthagar – she makes the gift of poetry:

To place on your simple gravestone,
calm in the cold air, I bring a poem
about truths. I wrote it with silences.

Writing against the backdrop of state-led atrocities and amnesia, civil war and censorship – through her particular poetic brand of spilling secrets and intimacies, embodying silences and spectres – she speaks truth to power. The sound of her poetry is loud enough – one need only be willing to listen.

Where Anar's poems are softly spoken and subtle, Carson is straight-talking and often sharply outrageous – illustrated in shouty capitals and suffused with ink. She assumes prior knowledge on the part of the reader, but also evokes the spirits of literary greats such as James Baldwin and Samuel Beckett, among others.

> DAY AFTER THE WAR –
> A DAY AS LONG AS THE REST OF THEIR LIVES FOR
> SOME...

> Poseidon laments –

> I LOVED THIS PLACE.
> THEN CAME THE GREEKS.
> CAME ATHENE.
> CAME THE TROJAN HORSE – YOU KNOW ALL THAT.
> *IT WAS SO MUCH KILLING.*

The goddess Athena – depicted as a pair of overalls with an owl mask – admits that although the Trojans were once her enemies 'NOW I WANT TO CHEEK THEM UP AND GIVE THE GREEKS A REALLY BAD VOYAGE HOME'. Full of such contemporary colloquialisms and expletives – alongside adhering to more formal conventions of Greek drama, such as choruses and soliloquies – Carson's project stands out for its defiant and deliberate world- and character-building – both wild and whimsical. In tow with Bruno's bold and detailed illustrations, from the mug shots to the fonts, it's a striking collaboration. Carson turns the genre of tragedy on its head, only to gesture at other, often invisible, forms of tragedy throughout history.

Carson is not an obedient poet and translator; she is a breaker of rules and codes. Her female characters – enslaved, engulfed in grief – too, bend, then break, societal expectations around femininity. At one point, Herald Talthybius (a raven), relays the prize for perfect feminine obedience: 'BE NICE, KEEP QUIET, RESIGN YOURSELF | YOU'LL STILL BE ABLE TO BURY THE CORPSE OF YOUR CHILD'.

Shape-shifters and loud speakers, the female characters refuse silence and refuse their suppression or suffocation as patriarchy and tragedy plays out. Their polyphonic chorus, composed of cows and dogs, bounces off the page ('WHOSE SLAVE WILL I BE?' 'WHOSE SLAVE WILL I BE?'); the pitch of their 'NO' 'NO' 'NO' is loud and clear, filling up panels on the page. Enough is enough. 'SAY WHAT YOU NEED TO SAY', shout the Daughters of Troy – to themselves, and to each other. Listen to our whispers, our wails, they rise up and demand readers. Despite it all, 'WE GO ON', they say, and sail into the distance.

Lines of Desire

Katy Evans-Bush reviews *To Love a Woman* by Diana Bellessi, translated by Leo Boix, Poetry Translation Centre, 2022 and *The Invisible Borders of Time: Five Female Latin American Poets*, edited by Nidia Hernández, Arrowsmith Press, 2022.

These two books together showcase a generation of South American feminist poetry, featuring the work of six poets born between 1941 and 1960. The oldest, Diana Bellessi from Argentina, published her first book of poems in 1972, the year before Adrienne Rich's *Diving into the Wreck*. In an afterword to this selection of her work, *To Love a Woman*, Mary Jean Chan writes about the poetic kinship between these two poets, for whom 'the personal is political'.

Diana Bellessi spent time in New York City in the early 1970s, working in a factory, teaching herself English, and translating the poetry of her US contemporaries. Years later, in 1984, she published Adrienne Rich in an anthology. Bellessi's poetic form, like Rich's, is a very loose, free verse that floats around the page, both delicate and – like a spider web – very precise and strong. The title poem, printed parallel over 22 pages, sexy, intimate, almost whispered, is addressed to the object of desire. It covers immense territory in few words. Myth narratives, language and touch – the differences between them, and the melting of one into the other.

Don't send me to the corner

Don't make of me a witness
that watches themselves [*que se mira tocarte*] touch you with words.

It is the named hand
not the name
that desires to hold your buttocks

    — Talk to me
    — How will it be?
    — *What?*
    — Your voice

    Hidden fire in the wood
    of fire that expands?

    Like this?
    The body in your voice
    the instant in which

don't send me to the corner

    honey flows from pomegranates

I don't want to
touch a ghost

The book is beautifully translated and introduced by Leo Boix,
who clearly feels a deep kinship with Bellessi's work, its form, its
musicality and its politics. As with the five poets in the new
anthology *The Invisible Borders of Time*, it's impossible to represent
such a poet in such a short selection. But what a gorgeous thing this
little book is! Give someone a copy soon. And how nice it is to see an
A-format paperback. Let's have more of these pleasing little volumes.

Mary Jean Chan writes that Bellessi 'explains that her love of writing, and of poetry in particular, is "the love of sustained contemplation".' This feeling sets the tone also for *The Invisible Borders of Time*, which features five major Latin American women poets from different countries.

In her short, almost clinical poems, the Colombian poet Piedad Bonnett tweezers the grief she lives with since the death of her son by suicide in 2013, and exposes its constituent parts to the air. 'What is terrible is not the abyss, but the edge' ('Edge'). In the original Spanish, the staccato music of her language gives nothing to romance:

> Pinté un perro para que cuidara mi puerta,
> un perro triste y feroz al mismo tiempo
> que disuadiera a cualquier atacante.

In Yvette Siegert's translations, the poems come across as matter-of-factly as those of Denise Riley, working on similar ground in English, with an utter lack of self-pity. It's grief as life. 'There is no scar, however gruesome', she writes, 'that doesn't also enclose some beauty. | A specific story is spun inside it...' ('Scars').

In contrast to Bonnett's work, Venezuelan poet Yolanda Pantin's has an almost public feel: 'Mosaic of the Single Woman' opens the section, and externalises feeling into almost a pronouncement:

> You know about a woman that she's single
> because she walks like a woman who's single
> You know she isn't expecting anyone
> because she walks like a woman who's not expecting anyone
> ...
> Single women don't inspire pity

Except that this poem seems to. It's forensic, though:

> The woman who thinks her singleness is curable
> is not a single woman
> it's a transitional state between two solitudes
> infinitely more dangerous

Notes for a Poetic ('Version II, against myself' is framed around a visit to visit the poet's sister in Paris, still seeing herself from the outside, 'two foreign women in the metro'):

> possessed as I was
> by a gallery of ghosts I devoted to them
> *the best years of my life*
>
> Shipwrecks storms Turners
> old prints that the bombing
> destroyed
>
> Wars do not discriminate
>
>   Madame X
>
> Today Persia
> tomorrow the river Ouse...

And 'Translating Ourselves', a sort of hymn to hesitancy ('Minimal gestures and minimal words that calm a little') seems to pull these strands together:

> There's something extraordinary
> in the place of Not Understanding
> and the desire to understand.

There's an almost journalistic feel to this fragmented mirror, as translated by Rowena Hill.

Carmen Boullosa is also a prolific and important novelist, essayist and playwright, and the author of *A Narco History: How the United States and Mexico Jointly Created the 'Mexican Drug War'*. Her concern with Mexico's identity, and its role in the imagination of the world, is evident in her poetry – as in this short poem, 'Patriots', given in its entirety:

> At gun point, fat and poor, your heroes go, fed up with Doritos
> and Cheetos, Mamaland;
>
> your palm trees bent in the breeze,
>
> drunk from the wind to the point of falling over,
>
> blown down by Hurricane Whichever;
>
> your petroleum wells capped off (when they aren't in criminal
> hands);
>
> your kidnap industry's booming
>
> to pay your way;
>
> gunshot music in the chests of children,
>
>> and still, the delicate bite
>
>> of a chili pepper in your perfect salsa.

Her love poems, as translated by Catherine Hammond, are dreamy and lyrical.

Rossella Di Paolo's poems are dreamlike in a different way from the others in the book: less autobiographical than any of the others, and more magic realist. Her poems are more concrete in their imagery; they feel like very sophisticated naïf-style paintings where animals and other elements of the natural world behave in unpredictable ways:

It's all right, sea.

I've seen you pick up your waves and stare at them. ('The Flight')

Cristina Peri Rossi's first poetry collection, *Evohé* – a depiction of
women's eroticism – caused an uproar when it was published in 1971.
She dived straight into, not the wreck, but something gloriously
unwrecked. Her 1975 collection *Descripción de un Naufragio* (Description
of a Shipwreck), includes this untitled poem, translated here by
Sophie Cabot Black and María Negroni:

> It was not our fault we were born into times of misery.
> Times of setting out to sea and navigating.
> Moving off in disturbances, in ships
> running from war, from tyrants
> toward the pendulum
> toward the swaying sea.
> He who carried the letter took refuge first.
> Wet letter, it was daybreak.
> From somewhere we saw the sea coming.

Peri Rossi's ten poems in this book are presented by three translators:
Sophie Cabot Black and María Negroni, Alexandria Hall, and Arturo
Desimone – the last of whom has translated seven of them. His
translations depart problematically from what Peri Rossi wrote, both
in meaning – *armador* means 'ship-owner', for example – and in tone,
where he uses words like 'atremble', heightening the register out of
keeping with the poems. There are examples in every poem, but in
'Desire' a pronoun is judged wrong – it must be 'he', as the poem is
about Tom Waits, not the 'she' in this translation. It's hard to see
how 'presagios', as in 'the night is full of portents', had to become

'soothsayings'. In 'To Live Twice', 'para acariciar tus senos' becomes 'to caress your bosoms'. 'Senos' means breasts. 'Bosoms' is simply egregious. Is it that the translator's Spanish isn't up to the job, or his English? Or that he's fallen prey to that force HG Wells apocryphally identified – that 'No passion in the world is equal to the passion to alter someone else's draft'? Whichever, it casts a shadow on the whole project – but as far as I can tell, the other translations are all beautiful, and some of the translators are as distinguished as the poets themselves.

There are other signs of sloppy production: typos littered throughout, inconsistent typography and punctuation, and what appears to be a formatting error on page 145. In the advance PDF at least, it seems the authors' documents were just poured in and never proofread as a whole manuscript. It wouldn't have taken a lot to have made this a much more lovely and careful book. Despite these issues, this poetry is self-evidently beautiful, important, world-class work by women whose voices add not just to the Latin American canon but also to the body of feminist and political poetry, and not easily available in English. The book is worth buying on those grounds, but in the case of Cristina Peri Rossi it will help if you can read some Spanish.

NOTES ON CONTRIBUTORS

HANIF ABDURRAQIB's most recent book, *A Little Devil in America: Notes in Praise of Black Performance*, was shortlisted for the National Book Award. Abdurraqib was awarded a MacArthur Fellowship in 2021.

AMRAN MAXAMED AXMED is a Somali poet, author and journalist who was selected by the Finnish Refugee Coundil as 'Refugee Woman of the Year' in 2005. She now lives in London.

LOUKY BERSIANIK (1930–2011) was a groundbreaking Québécoise feminist writer. Works include her legendary satirical, and witty, novel *L'Euguélionne* (1976, translated Howard Scott 1999), and a wealth of essays, essay-fiction, and poetry, notably *Maternative* (1980), *Axes et Eau* (1984) and *Kerameikos* (1987).

LEO BOIX is a British Latinx poet. He was the recipient of the Bart Wolffe Poetry Prize and the Keats-Shelley Prize. *Ballad of a Happy Immigrant* (Chatto & Windus, 2021) is his debut English collection.

HELEN BOWELL is London-based poet whose debut pamphlet *The Barman* was published by Bad Betty Press in 2022. She is a co-director of Dead [Women] Poets Society and a Ledbury Poetry Critic.

JULIA CIMAFIEJEVA is the author of three poetry collections in Belarusian. Her book *Motherfield* is forthcoming in the English translation from Deep Vellum Press. Born in the village of Spiaryzzha in the south of Belarus, she currently lives in political exile.

JOHN CLEGG works as a bookseller in London. His third collection, *Aliquot*, is forthcoming from Carcanet in September.

ASHA JAMA DIRIYE (1940–2004) was a singer, poet and actress, born in 1940 in El-Afweyn.

TOVE DITLEVSEN (1917–1976), one of the most notable Danish literary personalities of the twentieth century, wrote more than 30 books, including the memoirs of the recently published *The Copenhagen Trilogy*.

ALI OSMAN DROG was a distinguished Banaadiri abwaan (wiseman). He came from the same lineage as many other eminent Banaadiri abwaans, such as Aweys Geedow Aw Diinle and Macow Aw Diinle. He was famous for composing many of the heeso (songs), gabayo (poems) and geeraarro (poems) for the Banaadiri plays performed in the National Theatre in Mogadishu.

SASHA DUGDALE is translator of Maria Stepanova's *In Memory of Memory* (Fitzcarraldo, 2021) which was shortlisted for the International Booker Prize.

SARA ELKAMEL is a poet and journalist living between Cairo and NYC. She is the author of the chapbook *Field of No Justice* (African Poetry Book Fund & Akashic Books, 2021).

KATY EVANS-BUSH is a poet, blogger and critic. Her recent poetry publications are *Broken Cities* (Smith | Doorstop), and *Forgive the Language: Essays about Poetry & Poets* (Penned in the Margins). She is writing a book on hidden homelessness for CB Editions, and is a freelance editor and poetry tutor. katyevansbush.com, katyevansbush.substack.com

KATIE FARRIS is the author of *Standing in the Forrest of Being Alive* (Pavilion Poetry, 2023). Her writing and translations appears in *Granta*, *The Nation*, and *Poetry*.

NATASHA KANAPÉ FONTAINE is an Innu poet from the community of Pessamit on the North Shore of the St. Lawrence River. She is a slam artist, actor, visual artist and activist for Aboriginal and environmental rights.

MICHAEL FAVALA GOLDMAN (b.1966) is award-winning author of four books of poetry and translator of seventeen books of Danish literature. He resides in Florence, Massachusetts. https://michaelfavalagoldman.com/

SANA GOYAL is a writer and editor based between Birmingham and Bombay. She is the Deputy Editor at *Wasafiri* magazine and the Marketing and Outreach Officer at *Poetry Birmingham Literary Journal*. Her work has appeared in the *Guardian*, the *Los Angeles Review of Books*, *Poetry London*, *PBLJ*, *Wasafiri*, *Vogue* India, and elsewhere.

CYNTHIA GRAAE is a widely-published author of fiction, nonfiction, and translation. She is currently working on a collection of stories. She lives in New York City and Hiram, Maine.

W.N. HERBERT has worked with Said Jama Hussein and Maxamed Xasan 'Alto' on translations of Maxamed Ibraahin Warsame 'Hadraawi', among others, and 'Alto' and Martin Orwin on Maxamed Xaashi Dhamac 'Gaarriye'. With Said Jama Hussein he edited *So At One With You: An Anthology of Modern Somali Poetry in Somali*. He has co-translated from a number of other languages, including Bulgarian, Chinese, Dutch, and Farsi. He is Professor of Poetry and Creative Writing at Newcastle University.

IBRAHIM HIRSI is a student and writer. He works as a project assistant for YARD Art house and as an editorial assistant for PBLJ. A digital Somali cultural archivist and independent researcher, his writings explore the cultural changes that have occurred in Somali territories due to colonialism. His work is forthcoming in Flipped Eye anthology *Before Them, We* and he has worked as a consultant on Asmaa Jama's interactive short film 'Before We Disappear'.

FADUMA QASIM HILOWLE is a famous Somali singer who had a distinguished career. She worked on Radio Mogadishu in which she anchored many shows including a show called 'Imaqashii Imadadaali'. She regularly performed in the National Theatre in Mogadishu and was part of the famous Somali troupe Waaberi who performed both nationally and internationally.

SAID JAMA HUSSEIN was a founding member of Somali PEN Centre, and its vice-president until 2010, and is also a well-known Somali scholar, essayist and short-story writer. His first collection of short stories, *Shufbeel*, was published by Ponte Invisibile in 2010. A second collection,

Safar Aan Jaho Lahayn (A Flight into the Unknown), appeared in 2013. He has also translated a number of Chekhov's stories into Somali. He is fluent in English, Arabic and Somali and heads the translation section of the Redsea-online Cultural Foundation.

ASMAA JAMA is a Somali artist and poet, filmmaker and co-founder of art collective Dhaqan Collective, based in England. They have been published in places like *The Poetry Review*, *Magma* and *Ambit*. Asmaa was twice shortlisted for Brunel African Poetry Prize, shortlisted for the Wasafiri Writing Prize and longlisted for the National Poetry Competition. Asmaa is a Cave Canem Starshine and Clay Fellow.

ILYA KAMINSKY is the author of *Dancing in Odessa* (Faber) and *Deaf Republic* (Faber), which was shortlisted for TS Eliot Prize.

MONA KAREEM is the author of three poetry collections and three book-length translations. Her work has been translated into Farsi, Turkish, French, English, Spanish, Dutch, and German.

MAŁGORZATA LEBDA, ultramarathon runner and photographer, has published six poetry collections, which have won major Polish literary prizes. In September 2021 she ran along Poland's longest river, Wisła (a distance of 1113 kilometres) to draw attention to the environmental fragility of all rivers.

RAGIP LUTA is a co-founder of FLO, Kosovo's international Festival of Literature in Orllan. He was an editor and producer for the BBC World Service in London for two decades and has headed the BBC Albanian Service.

AMANI M is a self-taught digital artist based in the UK, reconnecting with her cultural heritage through a visual language that explores national identity. See her work at @4nine2

OLIVIA MCCANNON is a writer, translator and researcher interested in new ways of being and making on a damaged planet. www.oliviamccannon.com

VALZHYNA MORT is the winner of the Griffin Poetry Prize for her most recent poetry collection, *Music for the Dead and Resurrected* (FSG, 2020), now out in the UK from Bloomsbury.

KATRINA NAOMI won the 2021 Keats-Shelley Prize. Her third collection is *Wild Persistence* (Seren, 2020) and Katrina's recent collaboration with Helen Mort is *Same But Different* (Hazel Press, 2021). Katrina is learning Kernewek/Cornish.

MERET OPPENHEIM (1913–85), a Swiss artist, was one of the few women among the Paris Surrealists of the 1930s, best known for her objet d'art, 'the fur-lined teacup' (1936). Her collected poetry was published in 1984 by Suhrhamp Verlag under the title Husch, husch, der schönste Vokal entleert sich (Quick, quick, the most beautiful vowel empties itself).

MARTIN ORWIN is associate professor at the University of Naples 'L'Orientale', where he teaches and researches Somali language and literature. He has made translations of both early and modern Somali poetry for a number of publications.

HIBAQ OSMAN is a London based Somali poet. Her debut poetry collection *where the memory was* (2020) was published by Jacaranda Books as a part of their #Twentyin2020 initiative. She is a proud member of Octavia Poetry Collective.

AL PANTELYAT is a poet and translator from Kharkiv. His work has appeared in *Novaya Yunost, Deti Ra, Krechyatik*, and other publications.

MADELEINE PULMAN-JONES is a poet, writer, and translator. Her poems and prose have appeared in publications including *PN Review* and *The Guardian*. She is currently based between the UK and Poland.

LI QINGZHAO (1084–1155) was one of the most famous female poets in Chinese history, and lived in the Song Dynasty.

PAMELA ROBERTSON-PEARCE is a filmmaker, editor and translator raised bilingually in Stockholm. Her films include IMAGO: Meret Oppenheim. She has translated Swedish poets including Athena Farrokhzad, Ann Jäderlund, Magnus William-Olsson, Katarina Frostenson and Eva-Stina Byggmäster.

AISHA KARAMA SAED was born into an illustrious family known for their contribution to Somali arts and culture; her grandfather was the famous patriot and singer, Qasim Hilowle, and her mother, the famous singer, Faduma Qasim Hilowle. Aisha, like her grandfather and mother, has also been involved in Banaadiri music and culture from a young age.

AYAN SALAAD is a literary scholar, poetry enthusiast and translator of Somali poetry. She completed a PhD at Southampton University which compared expressive culture in Banaadiri oral poetry with globally circulating Indian Ocean texts. As part of the PhD, she recorded, transcribed and translated over twenty-five Banaadiri oral poems; creating an archive of traditional work songs, cultural poems performed during festivals and wedding songs.

HOWARD SCOTT has translated works by various Canadian poets, as well as novels and non-fiction, sometimes with his co-translator Phyllis Aronoff. He has twice won the Governor General's Literary Award, in 1997 for *The Euguelion*, by Louky Bersianik, and in 2018 with Phyllis Aronoff, for *Descent into Night* by Edem Awumey.

ANNA SELBY is editor of the anthology of erotic poetry *O* (Hazel Press, 2021). Her chapbook *Field Notes*, written mainly in and under the Atlantic Ocean using waterproof notebooks, was on the LRB Bookshop's Bestseller's List for 6 months. She is doing a PhD at Manchester Metropolitan University on Empathy, Ecology and Plein Air Poetry.

PRIMO SHLLAKU is an Albanian author, born in the northern town of Shkodër, in 1947. His first volume of poetry, *Flowers of the Night*, came out in 1994. Since then, he has published several other volumes of poetry. Shllaku is also known for his translations into Albanian of Baudelaire, Balzac, and Kafka.

DANA SIDEROS is a playwright artist and illustrator who has published two books of poetry.

TANYA SKARYNKINA is a Belarusian poet, writer and essayist. Her collection of short stories *A Large Czesław Miłosz with a Dash of Elvis Presley* is published by Scotland Street Press (2018)

ELŻBIETA WÓJCIK-LEESE writes with/in English, Polish and Danish. *Night Truck Driver* (Zephyr Press, 2020), her selection from Marcin Świetlicki, finalist for the Big Other Book Award for Translation, was longlisted for the 2021 PEN Award for Poetry in Translation.

RAAGE UGAAS WARFAA, who lived during the nineteenth century, was one of the most important poets in the history of Somali poetry.

XASAN DAAHIR ISMAACIIL 'WEEDHSAME' is widely regarded as one of the most promising Somali poets of his generation. He teaches literature at the University of Hargeysa.

AMANDA WONG works in consulting. She learnt to read and write Chinese in summer 2013 as a hobby and has had an interest in Classical Chinese poetry since.

LI YU (937–978), King of the Southern Tang Dynasty, is one of the most famous writers and early exponents of ci poetry.